First published in Great Britain in 1981 by
Frederick Muller Limited, London NW2 6LE

ISBN 0 584 10432 4

Every effort has been made to contact the
children who wrote the letters in this
book, but it was not possible in all cases.
The names and ages of the children are
included where they are known.

Cover artwork by Kathy Soulsby, age 6.
Cover design by Colin Lewis

Printed in Great Britain by Fakenham Press Limited,
Fakenham, Norfolk

# Dear Santa

a collection of children's letters to Santa Claus compiled by Stan Jones

Frederick Muller ltd. London

Every year thousands of children write to Santa Claus. This selection was chosen from over 8,000 letters sent to Jim Gilmour. It all started ten years ago when Jim pretended to be Santa to a blind boy. The boy was so captivated that Jim decided to start his dial-a-Santa service. As the calls flooded in to Santa's home at the North Pole (somewhere near Liverpool), the emergency lines became blocked, and the desperate G.P.O. asked him to stop. Jim wanted to help deaf children too so he began to invite and answer letters to Father Christmas.

Now Santa has opened his postbag to show us how touching, sad, thoughtful, funny and generous the children have been. These letters, mistakes and all, are direct and heart-warming, illustrated by the children's own evocative drawings. Some of their requests are simple, some are impossible, but they all demonstrate how important Santa Claus is, for in the words of one child, 'Christmas is the best fing in the world'.

Special thanks to all the children who wrote to Father Christmas and made this book possible.

and a Happy new. 🔴 year

Happy Christmas

Happy Christmas

and a Happy new 🔴 year

Dear Santa
            My Name is susan
an my age is eight years
old there is 15 in my family
and wee get nothing for Chrisbu
and everybody gets lots of thing
We get nothing no clothes or
toys and I would like you
to send me a real watch
and a per of felers th trouses
And a velet Jacket and a per
of shoes please my father
almost parlised and he gets
no were my mother is no well
and wee get no money or nothing
If you send me lot of things
and things for my bothers and
sisters I you will write back
            I have three bothers
is in gile and the get nothing
I never get up to see them

because I have no clothes
and no toys to play with
and I have two married sister
and they wont come near me.
And this is the names of may
brothers ans sisters paul, Colm,
carry, mariom, and me benny,
Kathleen, Roseleen lily, Micheal,
francis, Geara, James, Rolson,
and Tony. Please send me on
things

MERRY X'MAS

I have droun a picher
for you

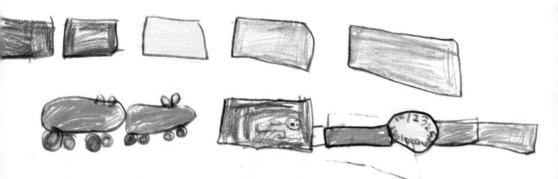

Dear Mr and Mrs Santa Claus. I
hope you are both well. This year I
would like ~~a pencil sharp 13J~~,
Sparkly ruched tube top 13J, a pair
of Jeans 15J or a signet ring.
I know I am asking for a lot
but I don't want anything else. Take
your choice.

Love Julie.
xx

SANTA CLAUS

anice        Drawing Makes me
happy.

Dear Santa
        You don't have to give me
    anything for xmas & Just leave
me    something for the other days.

ar father christmas

I am a good boy will
please bring me some
e track for my Train,
llingtons and a present
my dads
        friend
ildren he is in hosPital
got bad burnt in work
    lots of love
            Robert

Christmas is the best fing in the World

Dear Santa
        I love you. If you don't leave

me anything I won't cry. I am
a big boy now.

                P.S But I would be Very

    Sad

                                    Steve

To          Santa

Dear    Santa      at        christmas     you
have       to       go      around      the
world        with    all      the      toys
when        you      have    finished     you
must      be      tired.
            Sean

# DEAR SANTA

## CAN I COME TO YOUR HOUSE for a Holiday

Dear Santa,

please I dont want anything for christ[mas] I just want to make my mum[my] happy just for a few days. as our daddy left us all alone please can you send her a card just to make her happy again y you do sen[d] me a present I would like a book for drawing

all my love
Stephanie

I KNOW I have to be good to get presents and it was Jesus's birtday not just a day for playing.

Mark, 7

Dear Father Christmas,

Christmas will soon be here I can't wait. I hope I'm not too early writing to put my request in. I want girls Annul 2 Twinkle Annal, Secret 7 books not 1,5 and 2. The brownie annual and a digital watch.

See you some

From

Nicola

xxx

PS
Don't go near my mum because she got shingles)

PPS
We hope she will be better at Cristmas

Dear Santa,

Thank you for all the presents you gave me last year. This year I dont want alot my Mommy has been in hospital and i just want her to get better. If you could bring me a typewriter that would be very nice. I hope you have a nice christmas too,

love from
Ruthie ✗✗

Dear Santa
    My grandmother says that the best xmas
present is good health. I have good health
alralth already so I would like a doll

        Love gertude


I hope you don't get
    stuck in the snow and
If you do, I hope your
dears are strong enough
to pull you out.

Best wishes From JJ cavanagh


Send me a machine gun
and a box of stink bombs
I am pionning a surprise
for me big brother

Robert, 7

ar SANTA

am going too try my

st and help those poor

ittle children in cambodyer

uld you send them some

od and presants

Nancy, 8

I Like what you are
putting in My Stocking
because I Looked
at the top of the
coobend + I Saw them

Chris, 7

r santa,

My Favorite rabbit called Bunny would
like some lettuce + Brussel sprouts
because the one's you brought last
year have rotted now.

Greta, 8

Dear Santa
Do you were pillows in your
tummy or is that the real you

Dear Santa mummy say's
you will bring me a big suprise
as I am in hospital. Santa having
the Scars taken off my chin.

Sharon, 8

Dear Santa,
         Could you please make
a something nice for my wee brother
you see Santa he can not walk.
Santa he is a wee handicapped
boy. I would Love God to make
him walk so that he can play with
me Santa. I say my prayers
every night to God to help
my wee brother and he might
do it for christmas.
Santa if you come in the back
door in my house. I will leave
Fish and chip for you and a
drink of daddys wiskey
         Thank you Santa
              God bless you
         X X X X X X X X X X
         O O O O O O O O O

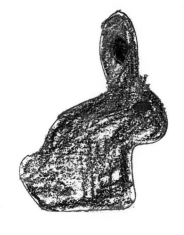

Dear Santa
hope you are well and giving the
Renda pleanty of oats whats the weather
like up there my dad says its brass monkey
weather down here.                Stephen, 8


Dear Santa

You are the onlyMan that works one day a year what do you do
all year round-does It get boring doing nothing at all

                    Love Lucy


Dear Santa
Could you do some magic to make
it snow on Christmas Day if I give you
one pound. Hope you and your reindeer
are well   Love Neil

Toy
Saok

Dear Santa I WONT
Leave you any mince pies
becuse you HAVE A
FAT Tummy AND you
jon't be able To get Down
A Chimny.
merry cHRISTm
JuLie

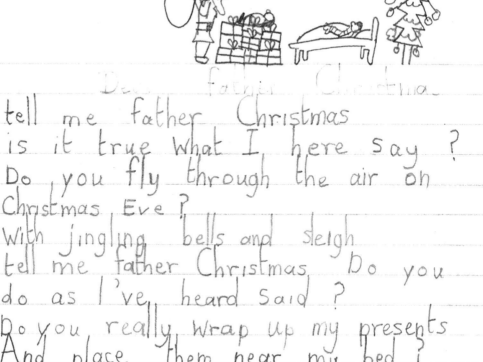

Dear Father Christmas

tell me father Christmas
is it true what I here say ?
Do you fly through the air on
Christmas Eve ?
With jingling bells and sleigh
tell me father Christmas Do you
do as I've heard said ?
Do you really wrap up my presents
And place them near my bed ?
Tell me father Christmas Does it
really make you sad ? When Children
grow up and then Say well it comes
from Mum - Dad .

Dear Father christmas
you didn't have any
portable tellys left, when you
came to Our house last
year, could you please
start at Our house first
this time.
We haven't got a chimney.
So don't forget to bring your
magic Key I hope you
liked the mince pie and cup
of milk what my mum left
for you I will leave a bucket
of wAfter for your randears
I LOVe you Father
Christmas.
    Love from Beverley
xxxxxxxx
    (x)

Dear santa

Give Rudolphs

nose an extra Polish so
he can find our house      Mary.

Dear sahta

my dad is un the
nick could you bring him home on

chrismas day      Peter, 7

Dear Santa I hope its not
true Cold at the north pole as
I wount Like you to catch Cold so
do what my dab tus and wara two pair
of socks

Dear Santa Claws

you are well I am. Do you reall I hope
go round the world at the speed o
light? Have a happy Christman
and new year
Love Stephen

Dear. Father Xmas,

my mummy says we cant go
to see nanny in London because my ba
brother has just come out of hospital, a
my daddy has got measles, all spotty.
Happy Xmas to you
Love Joanna
XX

Dear Santa I Would Like another
Grandad coz ive only got one.

Kathleen, 8

Dear Santa,
I am 7 and a half
and would like a new doll
for Christmas, most of all I
Would like my daddy home
to be with us all safeley
ao he is a Soldier and
is in Northern Ireland.
If you can will you give
my daddy and his friends
a nice present and big
Kiss for christmas
Thank you,
Vikki Joy
X

Dear    father    christmas
I       hope      it    is    all    wel
I       would     like  you   to     bring
me      a         doll's pram  because
  my    other     one   has    got   spides
and     crepy     croules  in   it.

Dear Santa if you have ~~an~~ ony overs
I will be very grateful.

John, 8

please father

Christmas

I want to be

a fairy
from maria
+ + +  + + +

It is nearly Xmas, starting. The bells, people go to the wishing wells, wish for a fotune and wish for fame. And I will wish for the Very best game. Xmas is coming its nearly here people are singing And full of good cheer 3 days to go I'mm rearly excited oooh its going so slow 3 days to go oooh its going so slow. and now xmas eve is here, mummy tells me go to bed theres a dear, father xmas will soon be here. lying in bed I'mm trying to sleep, thinking of presents. I hope to keep. I'vv bin so good and kind and sweet if I don't get what I want I'll kick daddy xmas in the teeth. good night.

# All MY Work
## DAWN

please may I have an
organ thank you, or else
you see I alwas have
~~good~~ bad look thats why
this note is funny.

please
take all the other
children a lot of
toys too especially
those with no mums
and dads luv you
from sarah age six

I like you

I support Tottenham, Peterborough and Ipswich.
I play for my school team. My position is left winger.
PS When I grow up I want to be a footballer
PPS I want to feel your white beard.
with love from
Julian
x x x x +x xx

Dear
Santa Daddy for
is gone
christmas to Heaven.
Love Noel.

Dear Santa

I don't believe in you. but my mum
and dad and my big sister do.
So can you send them some presants.
I don't want to spoil it for them
I am nearly ten. pehaps when I get bigger
I might believe in you like them. Have a nice
time pretending Robert, 9

I love you.
I wish I could see you
and the rain deers. but I
know I can not
Lots
of Love
From Macy

Dear Santa,

Bring my Dad a train set - he's always playing with mine.

John, 7

Dear santer

wold you Get my Dad
A Job Because he
is on the dole my
uncle is the dole my
mum works in a hospital

Karl 8

Dear SANTA My mum says I DONT
WASH be HIND My EARS E do its gust
That I DRy A FuNNy coloR bRiNg Me
LoTs OF ToyS

Robert, 8

Dear Father Christmas
I had helped my dad
Clen the Car but
evry time we start the
Car it brayes down. So
Pleas can I have Neutronic
man. From Clifford

could you plus please
tell how you
can get into my
house as we have
no Chimney
no Lone off from

Louise † † † †

Dear Santa,
Could you bring
me my twofront
teeth so I can eat
sweets if not false
ones will do till mine
come thruw

HAPPY X'MAS.

To Dear FatherChristmas
I hope you are
well, I am. I Love yo
and God very much. See
you soon,
love from
Sarah
aged: 6 years

Dear Santa,
My name is Kellie
and for christmas I would like
a doll's house, MAjoR Morgan,
a barber shop, and a new dolly
because I wrote on my other doll
and it won't come off.

Merry
Christmas

Dear Father christmas
          I hope your reindeer's
re ready for christmas   I would
ike a reindeer but I would not
ew were to keep it. I will
ang my Stocking up and put a
jamtart out for you. I hope
you have a happy new year.
  my mum would like an ice-cream
scoop.
          Love from Rebecca

♥ I love you

from alan

Lots of love and
Kisses and Hugs

love

lots of

love Kar

From Gary

All my love

Neil

xxxTtttTt

I like

father Christmas

xxxxxxx

xxxttttt

I love you santa, I
liked the toys that
you brought me last year
I remain
your fond friend
Seamus

Lo
An

mer

San

yo